ГРАДЪ.

...AGRAD,
...is MOSKVÆ

OCCIDENS · SEPTENTRIO · MERIDIES · ORIENS
Sapad · Sever · Letne · Stok

MAGNO DOMINO CÆSARI, ET MAGNO DVCI
ALEXIO MICHAELOVITS,
DEI GRATIA,

OMNIVM RVSSORVM AVTOKRATORI VLADIMIR..., MOSKOFS...
NOVOGORODSKII: TZAR KAZA... ...HANSKII, TZ...
SIBIERSKII: DOMINO PLESKOFS... ...NSKII, IVERS...
OVGORSKII, PERMSKII, VEATSKI... ...MINO, ET M...
NO DVCI NOVOGORODI IN TERR... ...TZERNIGOFSKII,
REZANSKII, POLOTZKII, ROSTOFSKII, IAROSLAFSKII, BÉLOZERSKII,
OVDORSKII, OBDORSKII, KONDINSKII ET TOTIVS SEPTENTRIONAL...
REGIONIS MANDATORI; ET DOMINO TERRARVM IVERSKYE,
KARTALINSKICHI, ET GRVZINSKICH CÆSARVM ET
TERRARVM KABARDINSKIES, TZERKASKICHI, IGORSKICH
DVCVM: ET MVLTARVM DITIONVM DOMINO
ET MODERATORI

Castellum cum tribus contiguis Vrbibus Moskuæ, prout
sub florenti Imperio, piæ memoriæ, Magni Domini Cæsaris,
et Magni Ducis Borissi Foedorovits, omnium Russorum, &c.
situ, et dimensu fuit; summâ ac debitâ observantiâ,
offertur, dicatur, consecratur.

In hoc Castelli Vrbis Moskuæ Typo hæc subsequentia suis numeris notata designantur ordine.

1. Podvorie, id est Porta Froloffskie.
2. Vofnesenie Monaster, Monasterium Ascensionis Christi, ubi Imperatrices sepeliuntur.
3. Aula Foedoris Ivanovits Selemeyteff.
4. Keriloffske podvorie, hospitium Keriloffskorum.
5. Kroetissche podvorie, hospitium Kroetisschorum.
6. Chobro duor, Armamentarium.
7. Roslono pricues, Tribunal aut Ius grassatorum.
8. Aula Ducis Ivan Vacilovits Siesskie.
9. Aula Ducis Foedoris Ivanovits Mofioslaffske.
10. Variæ Iuris Præfecture.
11. Pofolske: pricues, Peregrinæ Iuris præfectura.
12. Michael Archangel; Templum in quo omnes Cæsares sepeliuntur.
13. Porta ad ipsum flumen Moskua.
14. Gazophylacium Cæsaris, et Magni Ducis.
15. Blagavofsnie, Anuntiatio Mariæ; templum novem turribus, quarum tecta, ut et totius templi, ære deaurato coperta, sunt, imo et Crux altissimæ turris ex auro purissimo fabricata est.

16. Aula Cæsaris.   a. Novæ Aulæ structura.
17. Boeravnskevorod, Porta alta, sylva.
18. Commenemosf, Porta iuxta pontem lapideum.
19. Aula Patriarchæ.
20. Pretzisfa, Beatæ Mariæ Virginis, Soboorne tzurke, templum Synodale, quo Ecclesiastici omnes conveniunt.
21. Vetus Aula Domini, scilicet Borissi Fiedorovits Godunoff qui postea Cæsar fuit.
22. Troytzke podvorie; hospitium Troytzkorum.
23. Rofisfvie Christova; Templum in quo Cæsar, festo Nativitatis sacrum audit.
24. Ivan veliky; magnum Divi Ioannis templum, cuius turris tegmen deauratum est, campanis abundat.
25. Campana magna, pendens pene 2200. poedas, que valent ponderum nostratium 66000 libris.
26. Tzoudova Monaster; Monasterium miraculorum.
27. Aula Boydani Iadovits Bélskoy.
28. Aula Andreæ Petrovits Klesnin.
29. Aula Simonis Mikitovics Godunoff.
30. Aula Dimetri Ivanovits Godunoff.
31. Aula Gregorij Vacilovits Godunoff: postea fuit Granarium.
32. Nicoolske wrod; Porta Sancti Nicolai.

NEGLINA

FLVVIVS

Privilegio Nobilis
...rarum et Proprietatem
D. D. Ordinum...

THE WORLD'S CITIES

MOSCOW

CREDITS

Series Editor: Nicolas Wright
Series Designer: Kris Flynn
Picture Researcher: Kathy Brandt

Text and commissioned photographs by Deana Levin

Published by Chartwell Books Inc., A
Division of Book Sales Inc., 110 Enterprise
Avenue, Secaucus, New Jersey 07094

© Marshall Cavendish Limited 1978

Produced by Theorem Publishing Limited,
71/73 Great Portland Street, London W1N 5DH
for Marshall Cavendish Books Limited

Printed in Great Britain

First printing 1978

ISBN 0 89009 157 9

THE WORLD'S CITIES

MOSCOW

CHARTWELL
BOOKS INC.

CONTENTS

Introduction to Moscow

There is always a fascination in going to an entirely new place, but there is an extra fascination in going to Moscow for the first time, sometimes even, a slight feeling of mystery. Is there really an 'iron curtain'? Once there, however, it is clear that apart from the customs there has been no barrier to cross! The streets full of people, all with a sense of purpose; the colourful onion-like domes of the city's numerous little churches; the greenness of the squares; the boulevards and the courtyards behind the blocks of houses. These are some of the sights which introduce the visitor to this different world.

The Kremlin, the heart of the city, and the towers along its walls, can be seen from many points. The gate into the Kremlin is open and anyone can stroll in freely, roam its streets and gardens, enter a church or cathedral or look over the parapet wall down to the river below.

The Kremlin wall also forms one side of Red Square, another famous landmark in Moscow. No traffic is allowed here at any time, night or day. There are crowds of people, foreigners and Muscovites, who wander up and down, looking at the extraordinary Cathedral of St Basil, at Lenin's marble mausoleum, or at the windows of the large store known as 'GUM' which stretches along one side of the square.

The Moscow river, the Moskva, curves round in great sweeps and one can take a trip either on a swift hydrofoil or on a more leisurely river 'tram'. From the river there is a lovely view of the Kremlin domes and towers, with the Bell Tower of Ivan the Great rising above them all. Further up the river is the high bank covered by woods, and the Gorky Park. A walk up by paths through the woods leads to a platform at the top from which there is a panoramic view of the city, the loop of the river and the huge sports complex.

It is interesting to note that there are no private names over the shops. Instead, the inscriptions read 'Fruit and Vegetables', 'Food Shop', or 'Books'. Some of the clothes shops have names such as 'Svetlana', and a chain of children's shops is simply called 'Children's World'. There are also highly specialized shops like 'Cheese' or 'Tea and Coffee'.

There are no commercial advertisements in Moscow. Posters are put up on special boards showing the programmes of cinemas and theatres, or announcements of various exhibitions.

Russians love to eat ice creams at any time of the year and they are sold from stalls or kiosks along the streets as well as in cafes and restaurants. When the temperature is well below zero, the ice cream stalls are just as busy as in the summer.

The city looks very different in winter. For about five months there is not a spot of green anywhere. The snow comes down and the frost moves in and the bare trees look black against the sky. It is true that the snow ploughs keep the roads clear and the pavements are swept. The traffic moves freely, but the parks and gardens are covered and in the parks many paths are flooded and turned into skating rinks. In May the snow begins to melt and in no time at all the leaves are out.

Moscow is the capital of a vast country consisting of 15 republics. It is the gateway to many other interesting places, such as Samarkand in Central Asia or Lake Baikal in Siberia. So when you have seen Moscow it is easy to fly further and explore other parts of the U.S.S.R.

SADOVAYA-SPASSKAYA ST.

RUSSAKOVSKAYA ST.

CITY LANDMARKS

1. COMECON BUILDING
2. OLD UNIVERSITY
3. BOLSHOI THEATRE
4. LENIN MAUSOLEUM
5. TSAR CANNON
6. ST. BASIL'S CATHEDRAL
7. PUSHKIN ART MUSEUM
8. SPASSKY TOWER
9. ST. ANNE'S CHURCH/ROSSIYA HOTEL
10. ST. NICHOLAS OF THE WEAVERS CHURCH
11. TRETYAKOV GALLERY

5th OCTOBER ST.

RED
SQUARE

TCHKALOV ST.

YAOUZA   RIVER

MAURICE THOREZ
QUAY

ULIANOVSKAYA ST.

Origins and Growth

Moscow is one of the youngest capitals in Europe. It was first mentioned in an old chronicle in 1147 and this date has been officially taken as its foundation. The chronicle records that Yuri Dolgoruky (Yuri Longarm) sent an invitation to his relative, Prince Sviatoslav, to visit him in 'Moscov', where he had an estate. In 1156 Yuri fortified Moscow, which was situated on a hill between the Moskva River and the small, swift Neglinnaya River; Slav tribes had lived in this area for centuries as it was well placed for waterways and trade routes.

Archaeological finds have confirmed that in the twelfth century Moscow was a well established settlement with the fortress as its centre and the homes of artisans and traders outside the walls. Other discoveries of pots, ceramics and a seal of Kiev origin, from the same period, show that Moscow had contacts as far away as the Ukraine.

The first Kremlin walls were built of wood and enclosed wooden houses, a small wooden church and stables. Beyond the settlement were pine forests. In 1238 the Mongol-Tartars invaded Moscow and burnt it down. But it was rebuilt and became the capital of a small principality.

By the 14th century Moscow was the capital of a much larger area, that of the principality of Vladimir. Its growing importance was reflected by the fact that the head of the Russian Orthodox Church, the Metropolitan, moved to Moscow from the town of Vladimir.

In 1339 Prince Ivan Kalita, nicknamed Moneybags, extended the Kremlin, building new walls of oak. More traders, artisans and boyars (aristocrats) lived both within and outside it, on both sides of the river. Inside the Kremlin the first stone churches were built.

Around Moscow land was cleared of forest and planted with crops. Trade expanded and many of the great rivers were used, joined by porterage pathways; in this way it was linked to the Azov and Black Seas and to many inland cities such as Kiev.

From the time of Ivan Kalita, Moscow's rulers took the title of Grand Prince. Political and economic power increased and by the 15th century the city became the centre of the Russian people's struggle against the Mongol-Tartars.

In 1367 the wooden walls of the Kremlin were replaced by walls of white stone and fortified monasteries were built at strategic points near the city to strengthen its defences. The settlements outside its walls consisted mainly of artisans such as blacksmiths, potters, tanners, and armourers. At the end of the 15th century the stone walls were replaced by brick ones and extended still further. Eighteen towers were placed at the corners and along the walls of the triangular shaped fortress so that there were seven protecting each side. The walls were nearly 15 feet thick and they stand to this day.

Inside the Kremlin the cathedrals and churches were rebuilt and a new cathedral, the Cathedral of the Assumption was used for the crowning of the Grand Princes. Two palaces were also built.

The Spassky Tower on the Kremlin wall and St Basil's Cathedral from the back. The other side of the cathedral faces Red Square.

Left: Kolomenskoye Cathedral. Part of the outdoor museum on a former large estate on the bank of the Moskva River.

Below: Moscow fathers looking after their babies, enjoying the fresh air and their newspapers. Women's Lib. in action – Russian style.

As the settlements of artisans and traders spread further, they were very vulnerable to attack. Towards the end of the 16th century stone walls were built around these settlements, forming a second encircling ring. There were towers and gates through which radial roads led outwards beyond the city. Later, earth ramparts were thrown up beyond this ring; they were surmounted by wooden walls and towers. Some of the fortress monasteries were along this line of fortifications. A number of them still exist and are used as museums. The Inner Boulevard Ring and the Sadovoye Ring in present-day Moscow run where the second and third lines of fortifications were built. Parts of the second wall have been preserved; it was wide enough for a horseman to ride along it.

It was at this period that Ivan the Great's Bell Tower was built inside the Kremlin, and St Basil's Cathedral in Red Square. (Incidentally, the name Red Square is a mistranslation for Beautiful Square.)

As the city expanded, its unique circular shape developed. Radial roads ran in all directions from the centre, intersecting the ring roads which followed the lines of the walls.

During the centuries Moscow was not only attacked many times by the Mongol-Tartars, but also by the Poles and Lithuanians who plundered and burnt it in the 17th century, and by Napoleon, who invaded Russia in 1812. He was forced to retreat, however, when the Muscovites set fire to the city, having destroyed food supplies. When retreating, Napoleon's army destroyed buildings in the Kremlin and damaged the walls and towers. These were all restored later.

In the 18th century Peter the Great gave orders for the improvement of Moscow. He prohibited the building of new houses in the back yards of existing ones, ordering instead that they should be in lines facing the street. Stone pavements were to take the place of wooden walks and the whole city was to be 'modernised'. But as Peter became more and more engrossed in the building of what was to be the new capital, St Petersburg, not much of this plan was carried out.

Russia's first university, however, was founded in Moscow in 1775 by Lomonosov, the famous scientist after whom it is named. Theatres, as well as other educational institutions, were also built at this time.

Many street names and the names of squares in present-day Moscow still retain their connection with the people who lived there long ago. They recall the armourers, the potters, the cannon foundry, the cauldron makers and others. Some squares are named after the gates that once led into the old city through the towers on the fortification walls.

Above: The Tsar Cannon stands in the Kremlin grounds. It was cast by Andrei Chokhov, master of the cannon yard, in 1586.

Right: Friendship House, Kalinin Prospect was built at the end of the 19th century by the millionaire Morozov, who sent his architect to Portugal to study style there. There is a story that, when the house was finished, Morozov invited his mother, who lived in the country, to come and see it. When she looked at it, she is reported to have said: 'Till now, only I knew you were a fool. Now the whole world will know it'.

At the beginning of the 18th century Peter the Great transferred the capital from Moscow to St Petersburg. Moscow remained the industrial and commercial centre. Most of the nobility and the rich merchants moved to the new city and development in Moscow slowed down. Some of the nobility remained, however, and built themselves beautiful palaces in huge estates and laid out parks and gardens with grottoes, fountains, statues and pavilions. Many of these buildings stand today and are used by public organisations: for example, the former Pashkov Mansion is now part of the Lenin Library, almost in the centre of the city; others are used as the headquarters of the Academy of Sciences, the House of the Trade Unions (formerly the Noblemen's Club), and the Sklifosovsky Casualty Hospital.

In 1741 new city limits were defined by the building of the Kamer-Kollezhsky ramparts with 16 gates at which internal customs duties

Below: Some restored old churches near the Rossiya Hotel, near the bottom of Red Square.
Right: The Education Pavilion at the Economic Achievements Exhibition.

were levied on all through traffic.

By the end of the 18th and the beginning of the 19th centuries Moscow had a population of 275,000 and there were about 300 factories, many of them for textiles. After the defeat of Napoleon the reconstructed city grew even larger. It was at this time that the Bolshoi and Maly theatres were built. By the mid-19th century, when serfdom was abolished, artisans producing handicrafts were replaced by factory industries, though textiles still predominated.

Because Moscow's geographical position was so much better than that of the capital, St Petersburg, it was the centre of the development of the railways. Its population increased faster and it spread well beyond the Kamer-Kollezhsky ramparts, forming a new industrial ring. The 1897 census figures showed that the population was nearly a million strong.

The middle classes built themselves taller and bigger houses, four or more storeys high, near the centre of the city; these houses dominated the one and two storey wooden houses round them. The architectural style was very mixed, neo-classical, Romanesque, Gothic, pseudo-Russian and modern. The pseudo-Russian style imitated in stone the old wooden architecture. Compared with the dignified pillared mansions of the nobility of the earlier period, these are far less attractive than the buildings they emulate.

By the end of the 19th century the autocratic tsarist empire began to crumble and there was great unrest. The 1905 revolutionary uprising was crushed, but during the First World War, when Russia was losing, the poorly equipped soldiers were demanding an end to the fighting. They were asking for peace 'with their feet'. In 1917 the workers of Moscow joined with their brothers in St Petersburg and seized control. A year later the capital of the new Soviet state was moved to Moscow.

Left: The Church of St Simon Stylites, built in the 17th century, on Kalinin Prospect, holds its own among the tower blocks all around. It is now a museum belonging to the All-Russia Nature Conservation Society.
Above: Three young Muscovites in their courtyard.

In the early years after the revolution the country was torn by civil war, by wars of intervention and by terrible famine. Moscow, with the rest of the Soviet Union, remained little changed in its structure. Hundreds of lanes and little streets were still cobbled. The only way to house people with the greatest need was to put them into large flats abandoned by those who left the country, or in rooms considered surplus in large houses so that several families had to share kitchen and toilet facilities. Transport was limited, trams went through the centre of the city and choked the main streets when there was a power failure. Shop windows were empty. Everything — including food — was in short supply.

Plans were made for the future development of the city. The main radial roads had to be widened. As a preliminary measure to improve the housing situation, houses which were solid enough to stand it had extra storeys added.

It was found that behind the houses of what is now Gorky Street there was ample space to build new blocks of flats. Certain buildings of historic value were moved back by a method of underpinning. The present Moscow Soviet building (the equivalent to a local authority's headquarters) for example, was moved back 15 yards by this method. Subsequently it had two floors added on top. When the new blocks of flats in the yards were completed, the people in the houses in front were moved into them, as well as others from further away (they were much larger). The old houses were then demolished, leaving plenty of space to make the street into a wide thoroughfare.

The clusters of wooden houses around the former mansions of the rich industrialists and merchants had no running water. It had to be drawn from standpipes in the street. Heating was by stoves fed with wood and food was prepared on oil cookers.

Below: The former Moscow Stock Exchange, is now used as the city's Chamber of Commerce.

By the mid-1930s material conditions were beginning to improve, food supplies were increasing and housing was going up all over the city. But another terrible blow was in store – the Soviet Union was invaded and devastated by the Second World War.

The German army was so sure of capturing Moscow that they even transported marble with them to build new headquarters for Hitler in the capital! (This marble was later used to face a new building in Gorky Street.) But the people of Moscow built barricades across the approaches to their city and withstood the onslaught. By their heroic stand they won one of the greatest victories of the war.

The post-war period has been marked by large building projects. At first, fairly large blocks of flats were built, often with a certain amount of ornamentation on the outside; also the eight enormous wedding-cake skyscrapers, including the new university which dominates the city on the Lenin Hills, and the Ministry of Foreign Affairs. Then many five storey blocks, built around large courtyards and without lifts, were put up at great speed, often made of prefabricated parts which were assembled on the sites. More recently the City Soviet (Moscow's local government organ) decided to build upwards, and now tower blocks of varying heights are going up, especially in the new districts in the outer suburbs.

The small wooden houses are vanishing fast, their residents moving from their ill-equipped homes into modern flats with hot and cold running water, central heating and other amenities. In many places the only indication that a village once existed are the fruit trees and other old trees which have been incorporated into the greenery of the courtyards of the new blocks of flats. One of the first things that people do when moving into new places, is to plant trees and flowers in the yards; they also put up apparatus for small children and position seats where anyone may rest and enjoy the fresh air.

The Moskva River now has more than 20 bridges and is enclosed by granite embankments many miles long. Its water had been increased enormously by the building of the 80 mile long canal which links it to

Below left: The tomb of the Unknown Soldier is under the Kremlin wall just inside the Alexandrovsky Gardens. A perpetual flame burns in his memory.
Below: A sledge, or troika, as it is called, drawn by three horses. This one is used for joy rides in the grounds of the Exhibition of Economic Achievements.

the Volga, with pumping stations to ensure a regular supply.

The Neglinnaya River has long since been imprisoned in a conduit and runs underground into the Moskva. The same has been done to other small rivers. The only other river of any size in Moscow is the Yauza. It is a tributary of the Moskva, and in 1937 the rubbish was cleared from either side, its width nearly doubled, and its banks lined.

There is a complete plan for the future development of Moscow. Since there is no private ownership of the land in the city, there is no reason why it should not be carried out. It is hoped to make Moscow a model city with good living accommodation for all its citizens and every amenity possible. New housing is going up rapidly, but even so it will be a real problem to keep up with the needs of Moscow's growing population, now estimated to be more than seven and a half million.

Moscow is now among the largest cities in the world. It lies at the centre of the European part of the U.S.S.R., and is connected with the rest of the world by railways going in every direction, by airlines flying from four airports, by ships sailing to and from its river ports and by 13 highways. The plane only takes three and a half hours from Moscow to London and there are flights from Moscow to New York, Tokyo, Havana, Colombo and many other cities of the world. Trains go across Siberia in one direction and across Europe to the Hook of Holland and Paris in the other. It is also possible to go by car or tourist bus from most European capitals to Moscow, crossing the seemingly endless North European Plain.

Left: The Space Monument, 312 feet high, is made from titanium that shimmers in the light. Leading up to it is an avenue lined with the busts of scientists and cosmonauts involved in the space project.

Above: This statue of a worker and a woman collective farmer dominates the entrance to the Exhibition of Economic Achievements.

Moscow is the capital of an enormous country. It is its planning headquarters, it determines the distribution of industry throughout the territory of the U.S.S.R; this involves transport, agricultural development, the building of new cities, the opening up of new areas. It is also the seat of COMECON, the common market of the socialist countries.

Thousands of tourists from foreign countries visit Moscow every year; it can compete with any other capital in what it has to offer, historical places, sport, museums, theatre and ballet, concerts, interesting walks and trips on the river.

Traditional Moscow

With the sharp change in the political structure in 1917, old traditions were discarded and, over the years, new ones adopted. One that did remain, however, was the celebration of New Year; the kindly old man in a red, blue, or white robe, driving his reindeer through the air is called Grandfather Frost, but he behaves in the same way as Father Christmas does everywhere, bringing presents for both young and old and attending parties. His companion is a snow maiden.

Tall, decorated fir-trees are put up in many squares and other public places in the capital. The shops are decorated and sell special fare. Decorated trees appear in homes and at places of work; parties are held in schools, factories, clubs, homes . . . everywhere, just like other countries in Europe. Huge children's parties are held in the Kremlin and other large halls.

The Russian Winter Festival is held annually in Moscow from December 25th to January 5th. This is when the theatres and concert halls present special programmes for Soviet citizens and foreign visitors. The finest Soviet actors, ballet dancers and the most accomplished musicians are seen and heard during this period. As relaxation horse drawn troika rides are taken in parks, with hot tea from samovars provided on stalls along the way.

The other festival, the Moscow Festival of Stars, takes place in May. May Day and November 7th, anniversary of the Russian Revolution, are, of course, greatly celebrated. There are military parades followed by huge civilian demonstrations in Red Square and the whole city is decked with red flags and slogans. All the traffic stops until the evening and after the demonstrations people stroll leisurely through the main streets, buying snacks and ice cream at the stalls and enjoying family outings.

The first and last days at school now have their traditions firmly entrenched. On September 1st, (unless it is on a Sunday, when schools then start on September 2nd) around eight o'clock in the morning, hundreds of seven year old boys and girls may be seen walking along the streets with their parents, clutching large bunches of flowers. They are going to school for the first time and the flowers are a present for their teachers. Their teachers spend the first morning introducing the children to their new school. They are also welcomed by the top class, the tenth, whose members give each new pupil a gift, usually coloured pencils or some other useful objects.

The ceremony for school leavers involves the ringing of the 'last bell', when they officially hand over their responsibilities to the ninth class. There is then an evening dance and finally, at midnight, a walk in Red Square – the square is filled with young people in their party clothes strolling about until dawn.

Moscow's impressive October Revolution Parade demonstrates worker solidarity and the military muscle of the Soviet Union.

March 8th is International Women's Day, a day which in many countries is devoted to the question of gaining equality for women. As Soviet women have equal rights before the law, equal pay, equal opportunities in jobs and public life, its celebration is something of an anomaly. But as some of the old traditional attitudes of men towards women in the family still linger, the symbolic gestures made on this day towards women by men both at home and at work may be significant. Husbands, sons and brothers give presents and flowers to the women in the family, make the breakfast and wash up in the evening. At work, too, men present their women colleagues with flowers and there may be a festive cup of tea.

It is a custom for young people, after their wedding ceremony, to visit two places. They lay a wreath on the tomb of the unknown soldier in the gardens beneath the Kremlin Wall, and they go up to the viewing platform at the top of the Lenin Hills to look at the panorama of Moscow below. Then home to a big celebration party!

Above and left: The Lenin Mausoleum contains the embalmed body of Lenin. On the days when it is open to the public, queues of people line up to pay their respects. The top is used as a reviewing platform on May 1st and November 7th.

Above: Grandfather Frost with a school choir at a New Year celebration.
Right: Traditionally, on their first day at school, Moscow schoolchildren present their teachers with bunches of flowers.

The Kremlin's Glory

Every visitor to Moscow must see the Kremlin. This fascinating complex contains a fabulously rich collection of art treasures, churches and palaces dating from different periods, starting at the 15th century.

The word Kremlin means a high fortified place. It is entered through the gates of the Kutafya and the Troitsky towers, with the bridge over the former moat between. The first building inside is the most modern, the Palace of Congresses, finished in 1961. This is the seat of the Soviet Parliament, but the hall is also used for concerts and for performances by the Bolshoi Ballet and visiting companies.

There are many historic buildings in the Kremlin; the former arsenal, completed in 1736, has the guns captured from Napoleon's army mounted on its high, thick walls; what was once the Senate House is now the seat of the U.S.S.R. Council of Ministers; the Bell Tower of Ivan the Great rises 265 feet into the air, it dates from the 16th century and is crowned with a gilded dome. At the foot of the tower is a bell, weighing 200 tons and cast in the 18th century. It was never hung and was badly cracked in a fire when a huge piece fell off.

But the most beautiful part of the Kremlin is the square, which seems full of cathedrals and palaces. They are now preserved as museums, and contain frescoes, murals, icons, the tombs of tsars, and the throne of Ivan the Terrible.

There is a pleasant garden with seats, fruit trees and flower beds and a view over the ramparts down to the Moskva River.

A beautiful and powerful view of the Kremlin at night, its lights enchantingly reflected in the river.

Left: The gold-coloured cupolas
give a fairy-tale look to the
Annunciation Cathedral.
Above: The equally extravagant
Assumption Cathedral.

31

Left: Some of the elaborate frescoes decorating the walls of the Granovitaya Chamber in the Kremlin.

Above: An icon of 'Christ All-Seeing Eye', from the 14th century, in the Kremlin Assumption Cathedral.

Right: The 16th century fur-trimmed crown of the Kazan Kingdom is made of gold and studded with precious stones and pearls. It is exhibited in the Kremlin Armoury and was once worn by Ivan the Terrible.

Below left: The Tsar Bell, weighing 200 tons, was cast in 1733 but never hung. It was cracked in a fire in 1837 and a piece weighing eleven tons fell off.

Below: Lenin's study in the building of the Council of Ministers in the Kremlin. He used it from 1918 to 1922.

Right: one of the many paintings of Lenin. This is entitled *Lenin's Return to Russia* and is by K. Aksyonov.

Old Moscow

There are parts of old Moscow all over the city; some will vanish as reconstruction goes ahead; some will be preserved because of its historic and aesthetic value.

During the many battles and invasions in the history of Moscow, the houses, which were originally made of wood, were burnt down or gutted. Only the churches, which were of stone, remained to show the style and skill of the old Russian builders.

In addition to those in the Kremlin, there are numerous small and medium sized churches dotted around the city. Most of them have been completely restored and are often used as small museums. A certain number are still used for worship.

One of the oldest is the Church of Antipy, dating from the 16th century; the Church of Nikola-in-Pizhi is a fine example of 17th century Russian architecture, with a tent-like belfry and an ornate pyramid of rounded gables and domes. The Church of the Nativity-in-Putinki, near Pushkin Square, is an interesting 17th century church, built at the time of the stone fortifications around the city. It is impossible to walk in any direction without soon coming across one or other of the dozens of churches still standing.

Many of the great mansions which belonged to the aristocracy are now used as the headquarters of various organisations. They can be recognised by their porticos and the columns which support them. Merchants who wished to imitate the style were allowed only to have simulated columns fixed to the walls of their houses! (They did not always abide by this restriction, however.)

A few examples of this kind of architecture are: the present Rheumatism Research Institute, in the former house of merchant Gubin; and the Institute of Physical Culture in the former palace of Count Razumovsky, which was one of the few timber palaces which escaped the fires of 1812. It was built by an English architect. The Archive of Military History is kept in the palace of Franz Lefort, one of Peter the Great's admirals, and built at the end of the 17th century. Such buildings are found in all parts of the inner ring of the city. Their outside walls are still painted in the traditional colours, warm yellow, pale blue or pale green, often picked out with white.

As one would expect, the area near Red Square on the side away from the Kremlin, is full of old buildings. The street, now called 25th of October Street, was formerly part of Kitai-Gorod, inside the second line of fortifications and there is still a gate and part of the wall left. In the courtyard of number seven, there is part of the Monastery-behind-the-Icon; No 15 was the Printers' Yard, where the first printing press was set up in 1563. The first Russian newspaper was produced here in 1703. The building, with its lace-like carvings in white stone on the facade, is now the Institute of History and Archives.

Not far from this street are three squares next to each other, called New Square, Old Square and Nogin Square, with a very wide boulevard running along the side. At one end is the large Polytechnical Museum, which is a mixture of styles as it was put up between 1877 and 1907, parts being added at different times.

At the beginning of the boulevard is the Monument to the Grenadiers killed at Plevna during the Russo-Turkish war of 1877-1878. The Church of all the Saints-in-Kulishki, was built in 1380 to commemorate a victory over the Tartars, and was reconstructed several times, the last occasion taking place in the 17th century. Near by is the Church of the Trinity, also 17th century – beyond these squares, and all around the Hotel Rossiya are various churches which

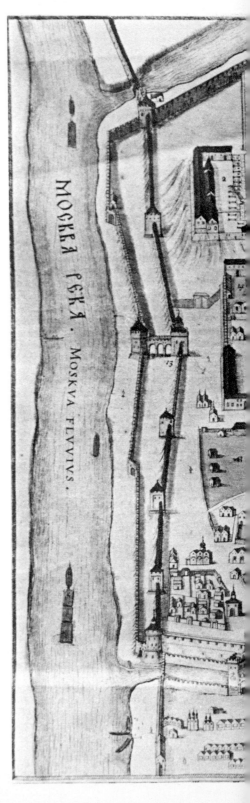

An early 17th century plan of the Kremlin.

КРЕМЛЕН ГРАД.
KREMLENAGRAD,
CASTELLVM VRBIS MOSKVÆ

MAGNO DOMINO CÆSARI, ET MAGNO DVCI
ALEXIO MICHAELOVITS,
DEI GRATIA,
OMNIVM RVSSORVM AVTOKRATORI, VLADIMERSKII, MOSKOFSKII
NOVOGORODSKII: TZAR KAZANSKII, TZAR ASTOROCHANSKII, TZAR
SIBIERSKII: DOMINO PLESKOFSKII: MAGNO DVCI SMOLENSKII, IVERSKII
OVGORSKII, PERMSKII, VEATSKII, BOLGARSKII: ETIAM DOMINO, ET MAG
NO DVCI NOVOGORODI IN TERRIS INFERIORIBVS, TZERNIGOFSKII,
REZANSKII, POLOTZKII, ROSTOFSKII, IAROSLAFSKII, BELOZERSKII,
OVDORSKII, OBDORSKII, KONDINSKII ET TOTIVS SEPTENTRIONALIS
REGIONIS MANDATORI; ET DOMINO TERRARVM IVERSKYE,
KARTALINSKICHI, ET GRVZINSKICH CÆSARVM ET
TERRARVM KABARDINSKIES, TZERKASKICHI, IGORSKICH
DVCVM: ET MVLTARVM DITIONVM DOMINO
ET MODERATORI

Castellum cum tribus contiguis Vrbibus Moskuæ, prout
sub florenti Imperio, piæ memoriæ, Magni Domini Cæsaris,
et Magni Ducis Borissi Foedorovits, omnium Russorum, &c.
situ, et dimensu fuit; summâ ac debitâ observantiâ,
offertur, dicatur, consecratur.

Above: A 17th century print by Vasnetsov showing the Kremlin's walled grandeur rising above the wooden houses of the city.
Left: A stone lion, part of the Spassky Tower's decorative features.
Right: The 16th century Church of St Anne. It stands near the river in front of the Hotel Rossiya and has been beautifully restored.

have been restored to their former beauty.

The Arbat is another area dating back to the old fortifications. Here there used to be a gate in the outer ring. In the 16th and 17th centuries artisans and craftsmen lived here and many of the still narrow and winding streets bear the names of their callings, such as silversmith, carpenter, bread and tables. In the 19th century aristocrats built their mansions in this district and many are now used by public bodies.

It is still possible to find wooden houses in some parts of Moscow, which, before the Revolution was known as 'the big village'. A few of historic value will be kept but the rest will vanish. Any traces of the villages that were engulfed as the city expanded will only be found in the names of the districts where they once stood.

Left: The intricately carved front gives this old Moscow farmer's house a distinctive appearance.
Above: A two-storeyed wooden house from another village now engulfed by the city. It will probably vanish as this part is rebuilt.

Below: A romantic view of Smolensk Cathedral situated in the Novo-Devichy district of the city of Moscow.
Right: One of Moscow's few remaining old buildings. Time has given it a crown of vegetation.

Along The River

Trips along Moskva River start at the Kiev pier and go downstream. On the slower river trams it takes about an hour and a quarter to reach the end of the route, going round two great curves.

The first sight on the left bank is of the fortress walls of the former Novo-Devichy Convent. Its fine belfry rises above the cupolas of the churches inside the walls. The convent dates from the early 17th century and the belfry was built in 1690. It was in the convent cathedral that Boris Godunov was proclaimed tsar in 1598. Later the wife and sister of Peter the Great were imprisoned there for plotting against him. Many famous people are buried in the cemetery within the walls.

Next, on the same side of the river, is the sports complex of Luzhniki and opposite, the steep high slope of the Lenin Hills come down almost to the water. At this point there is a double-decker bridge carrying the underground and a road over the river. There is a station actually on the bridge, with escalators going up towards the top of the hill. At the top, dominating the skyline, is the giant building of the Moscow University.

As the boat rounds the first curve of the trip, the gardens at the foot of the Lenin Hills widen into the large territory of the Gorky Park. On the left bank, beyond the embankment road, are many new buildings.

A succession of bridges span the river, most of them either reconstructed or built since the Revolution. The Crimea Bridge, just below the park, is a very long suspension bridge, and beyond it the new huge picture gallery to replace the Tretyakov, is going up.

At this point, on the left bank, stands a two storeyed house with a quaint roof, a large balcony of brick and an ornamented facade. It was built in the late 19th century. During the Second World War it was used by the French Military Mission and there is a plaque on the wall in memory of 42 heroes. The French airmen fought with their Soviet allies on the front from Moscow as far as Germany.

The Drainage Canal, which branches off to the right, was built in 1786 along the former channel of the river, which it rejoins further down. On the left are the high diving boards of the Moskva swimming pool. A little further down, up on the hill, the whole wonderful panorama of the Kremlin palaces and churches with their golden domes bursts into view. It holds the eye and tends to distract attention from some of the interesting buildings on the other side. One is a rare survival from the 17th century, a boyar's house, and next to it a church which has been restored. The British Embassy is a short distance further down.

On the same side as the Kremlin, down the river, is the huge Rossiya Hotel which can accommodate several thousand visitors; many Muscovites regret its position as it spoils the view from Red Square towards St Basil's. In front of the hotel is a small church surrounded by young trees.

Like most great cities, Moscow was founded on the banks of a river and, as a result, grew in size and importance. The River Moskva flows through Moscow and a trip down it is an ideal way to see the city.

Soon the boat reaches the place where the River Yauza falls into the Moskva. New parts of Moscow can be seen on either side and the last stop is at the Novo-Spassky Bridge, near the Novo-Spassky Monastery. This is one of the fortress monasteries and its towers and belfry can be seen above the walls.

From the same starting point as for this trip there are boats going up-stream, in the opposite direction. The river curves a great deal and the excursion ends at Fili-Kuntsovo Park and a river beach.

A ride on a hydrofoil along the Moscow-Volga Canal starts at the river port, Rechnoi Voksal, which is actually on the Khimki Reservoir. The boat passes through the pleasant countryside around the city, with a number of stopping places where people picnic, swim or sunbathe. There are many bathing beaches, boating centres, quiet corners for fishing and interesting small towns along the route.

Large steamers pass on their way down the Volga and since the opening of the canal, cargo-carrying boats can reach five separate seas from Moscow.

Below: Hardy Muscovites taking a Sunday dip in the Moskva.
Right: A hydrofoil trip along the Moscow-Volga Canal is an exciting way to see the city and parts of the surrounding countryside. The hydrofoil has a wake which folds in on itself, thus safeguarding the banks.

Left: Arkhangelskoye, near Moscow. Part of the estate is on the high bank of the Moskva River and has this kind of outlook.
Below: A view of the Lenin Stadium from across the river.

Sporting Moscow

Muscovites, young and old, like most Soviet citizens, are very keen on sport and have excellent facilities for any kind they choose. Many organizations, factories and the university, have their own sports clubs and between them have built around 70 stadiums in the city. In addition to providing for football games, there are usually facilities for other sports at these stadiums. Under the grandstands are gyms and other sports' rooms, showers, changing rooms, and a first-aid post. Certain times during the week are set aside for children's sections, with coaching from experts.

In a wide loop of the Moskva River is the huge sports complex of Luzhniki. It occupies an area of more than 350 acres and provides for almost every type of sport, games and athletics, both in winter and summer. Its central stadium is the largest in Europe; one section seats 103,000, another 15,000. The Palace of Sport accommodates 17,000 and is used for a variety of competitions such as gymnastics and figure-skating, as it can be converted into an ice-rink. All the buildings and pitches are set in a well laid-out park, where, in winter, parts are flooded for skating.

Football is enormously popular and matches are always sure of a full crowd as well as a huge television audience. The climate, with five months when the ground is covered in snow, means that football is almost a summer game. Ice-hockey, said to be one of the fastest games in the world, is played mostly in winter.

Swimming can go on all the year round. There are beaches along the Moscow-Volga Canal, and there are many swimming pools, both indoor and out. The giant Moskva swimming pool and the smaller Chaika are open all the winter and are, of course, heated. One can see the huge cloud of steam rising into the air above the Moskva from a long distance and the swimmers have to move about in a mist! As in other countries, in winter there are those hardy types who like to break the ice and plunge into freezing water. Holes are made for them and they have a special gala swim on New Year's Eve.

Holes are also made in the ice for winter fishing. People, huddled in warm clothing, sit for hours on stools waiting for the fish to come up to the holes to breathe. It is an extraordinary sight: a long stretch of ice with black dots of figures sitting all over the place! Fishing is also a summer pastime for many, both young and old.

Skiing is another popular winter sport. It is hard to find any steep and long slopes anywhere near Moscow. Nevertheless there is ample flat space in several of the large parks in the city. At weekends people can be seen setting off for the railway stations with their skis over their shoulders, bound for the countryside. There are centres both in the parks and in the country where it is possible to hire skis and boots.

Olga Korbut, world champion gymnast, is the winner of many medals. She is known throughout the world for her vitality and lively personality.

One of the features of Moscow, as it is indeed for the whole of the U.S.S.R., is the encouragement given to children to take up sports. There is one sports complex which belongs exclusively to schoolchildren. Many courtyards are flooded in winter and used by the children living there for skating and ice-hockey. The click of the hockey sticks against the puck can be heard as one goes along the pavements. Children begin to skate at a very early age and can join figure-skating classes at most stadiums.

There are competitions (called Olympiads) in all sports at every level. In this way the Soviet Union produces many fine athletes, gymnasts, and football and ice-hockey players. The costs to the individual are minimal as the state gives heavy subsidies and every help and encouragement.

Below: Three girl swimmers, the Olympic medallists, Koshevana, Russanova and Jurchenia. Russia is world-renowned for the skill of its sportsmen and women.

Right: The Moskva Swimming Pool. This enormous pool is round and divided into sections. It is heated in winter and the steam rising from the water forms a warm, protective layer of air for the swimmers. The rising steam can be seen for miles. The pool is entered from the changing rooms through an underground tunnel.

Left: Faina Melnik, the discus thrower.
Below: The Lenin Central Stadium is in the sports complex of Luzhniki, by the river. Its large bowl seats 103,000 and the other bowl seats over 15,000. Under the grandstands of the large bowl there are several storeys which provide for gyms, massage, medical rooms, dressing rooms, showers, snack bars and other amenities.

Left: This courtyard belonging to a block of flats has been flooded and is used as a rink by the inhabitants. This is a very common occurrence all over the city during the winter.
Above: Muscovites leaving the city on what is known as a 'health train', one of many used for weekend excursions to the country.
Right: Valeriy Borzov, 100 metre champion of the Soviet Union and an Olympic gold medallist.

Above: A fencing match at the
World University Games.
Right: A team of Russian gymnasts
displaying their skills in a human
column.

Shopping and Eating Out

Moscow shops, especially those near the centre, are so full of customers that it is difficult to get close enough to the counter to see what is on display. Tourists, if they wish, can buy souvenirs and other articles in their own currency, either at the special counters in their hotels (most of the big hotels have them) or in several special shops in the city, called Beryozka. The hotels also sell items in Soviet currency.

The quality and quantity of goods in Soviet shops is still not as good as those in, for example, London or New York, but some, such as books and gramophone records, are of good value. For those foreigners who do not know the language and wish to go shopping, there are always fellow customers pleased to help them over any difficulties they may experience.

The largest shop, or rather, shopping complex, is GUM (pronounced GOOM) in Red Square. This is a series of three parallel arcades on two floors, containing shops of every conceivable kind. In the centre of the middle arcade is a fountain, and here there is a very good souvenir shop selling handicrafts from different parts of the country: lacquered wooden articles, pottery, bone and wood carvings as well as many other items. Opposite, is a jewellery shop. The ice cream sold in GUM is delicious, as the number of people eating it proves!

TSUM is a large department store by the side of the Bolshoi Theatre. (TSUM are the Russian initials for Central Department Store.) On the ground floor there are several counters selling souvenirs. This shop also has branches further up the street, which is called Petrovka.

On Petrovka there is also a special shop selling traditional handicrafts of a very high quality and most attractively displayed. Kuznetsky Most is a street running into the bottom of Petrovka. It is full of bookshops.

Another good shopping centre is the new part of Kalinin Prospect, a wide street with very wide pavements. The street is lined with skyscrapers which hardly dominate because they are built somewhat back from the road. In this street is the largest bookshop in Moscow, a good record shop and a variety of other stores and also a number of restaurants.

Gorky Street was one of the first shopping centres in Moscow and is well worth a walk. Near the bottom is the Central Telegraph Office where the latest issues of the attractive Soviet stamps may be bought. Along this street there are some fine bookshops, many food stores, a Beryozka shop and shops selling clothes and materials.

In addition to the shops, on the pavements of the main streets there are numerous stalls and kiosks selling fruit, ice creams, newspapers, cigarettes and cheap souvenirs, kvass (a fermented thirst-quenching drink) in summer, theatre tickets, cakes and other things – they are often the overflow of shops, and, of course, they are all state-owned.

Beriozka shops can be found in most of the tourist hotels and in two districts of Moscow. They sell all sorts of goods, including souvenirs and handicraft items in exchange for foreign currency.

Left and above: GUM consists of three parallel arcades on two floors with a series of shops selling everything imaginable — food, materials, photographic supplies, clocks, records, haberdashery, stationery and, of course, ice cream which is delicious and rightly popular with the crowds who come to do their shopping here.

Every district in Moscow has a large covered market where collective farmers can sell their produce; the fruit and vegetables often come from their private plots. They travel from as far away as Central Asia with the kind of fruit that does not grow in a cooler climate, such as grapes, peaches and melons. There are also stalls run by state enterprises at prices found in the ordinary shops. Here in the markets are fruit, vegetables, milk products, meat, honey, plants and flowers. There is a big Central Market in Tsvetnoi Boulevard.

Moscow is not yet provided with enough snack and coffee bars, nor are there nearly enough quick service cafeterias, cafes and restaurants. Restaurants attached to hotels are usually open to non-residents. If one wants to have an evening meal in a restaurant, however, it is wise to go very early or to book by phone. When Russians go out for a meal it is with the intention of having a real outing, eating in a leisurely way, and dancing between the courses. They are apt to occupy their tables for the whole evening!

The restaurants of interest to foreigners are those providing food from the national republics; the best of these include the Aragvi, specializing in Georgian dishes, kebabs, spicy sauces with chicken, fish or cheese, and very good wine; the Uzbekistan, with special soups, its own kind of kebab, delicious flat bread and good wine. The Ararat serves Armenian food, the Baku, Azerbaijanian food and there are others serving foods from different republics.

Left: A Moscow bookstall, typical of many throughout the city. Stalls like these always attract large crowds.
Below: The interior of a large food store.

Left: The exterior of GUM, Moscow's largest store.
Right: Petrovka, a popular shopping street near the Bolshoi Theatre.
Below: Young people getting married have the choice either of a special ceremony in a wedding palace, where they can also celebrate in a special room with food and wine; or they can go to an ordinary registry office in their district. This is a last-minute-present shop in the palace itself.

Cultural Moscow

Moscow is a great cultural centre. There is far more than the world famous Bolshoi Ballet and the architectural riches of the Kremlin. The city has numerous museums, art galleries, theatres, cinemas, concert halls and historic sites, most of which are worth more than one visit.

The Tretyakov Art Gallery is based on a private collection presented to the city in 1892 by P. Tretyakov. The building looks like something out of a Russian fairy tale. It houses an enormous collection of Russian art, including the works of contemporary Soviet painters and sculptors. It is now far too small and a huge new gallery is in the process of construction near Gorky Park.

The Pushkin Gallery of Western Art contains a collection of classical and other sculptures, as well as many fine paintings, including early Italians, El Greco, Rembrandt, Constable, Corot, Picasso and van Gogh. The smaller Museum of Eastern Art houses carvings, jade ornaments, pottery and other handicrafts from China, Japan, India, Turkey, Iran and the Central Asian Republics of the U.S.S.R.

Many of the city's 28 theatres are of a very high order. The theatres have permanent companies, are heavily subsidized and work on a repertory programme. Some of them have their own acting schools. There are several theatres presenting ballet and opera; the Bolshoi has an opera company and two ballet companies, one of which performs in the Palace of Soviets in the Kremlin and the other in the Bolshoi itself. The Stanislavsky Theatre also has a ballet and opera company and its version of *Swan Lake* is different from that of the Bolshoi. The Moscow Art Theatre is well known for its presentation of Chekhov and other Russian classics while the Taganka Theatre has earned itself world fame for its experimental staging of a wide variety of plays.

The Central Children's Theatre next door to the Bolshoi, and the Theatre of the Young Spectator, as their names suggest, cater for different age groups of young people. The Central Puppet Theatre, with its intriguing facade, is popular with young and old alike.

Buying a ticket for almost any kind of production is difficult; Muscovites are keen theatre-goers, as is evidenced by the queues at the box offices. One feature of the theatre scene: all outdoor garments must be left in the cloakrooms. In the winter members of the audience bring shoes so that they can leave their thick boots outside and enjoy themselves in comfort.

Some of the 14 house museums are charming. These were the homes at different times of famous writers, composers, actors, artists and scholars, including Gorky, Tchaikovsky, Chekhov, Tolstoy and many others. These small old houses have been preserved intact amidst the tall new buildings.

There are other museums to suit all tastes: museums such as the History Museum on Red Square; the Lenin Museum nearby; the Museum of the Revolution on Gorky Street and the Museum of the History and the Reconstruction of Moscow, in the former church of St John under the Elm in Novaya Square. Part of the History Museum is in the former Novo-Devichy Convent, built in 1525, and enclosed by a crenellated wall with 12 towers.

This new section of Moscow University was completed in 1953. The central part of the building is 780 feet high, topped by a 200 foot spire. There are 37 buildings dotted about the 415 acres containing, among other amenities, 1,000 laboratories and 148 auditoriums. The library contains over one and a half million books. A large botanical garden and an observatory lie in the park which surrounds the university.

The Ostankino Palace Museum of Serf Art is unique. It was built in 1791-1797 in neo-classical style and is made entirely of wood. It was owned by the Sheremetov family, whose serfs, many of whom were superb artists and craftsmen, designed and built it. The moulded ceilings, the perfect proportions of the rooms, the chandeliers, the furniture and the parquet floors of rare woods are witness to their skill. The largest room in the house is the theatre, with a stage which could hold an entire company of 200 serf-actors. By a clever mechanism invented by one of the serfs, the seats in the auditorium could be moved in a few moments to clear the floor for dancing.

A number of former monasteries and churches are now museums of different kinds and several halls belonging to the Union of Artists hold temporary exhibitions of paintings and sculpture executed by contemporary artists.

The cultural scene in Moscow includes over 70 publishing houses, which produce millions of books yearly; cinemas; a fine circus; cultural clubs belonging to factories, enterprises and organisations, where their members can relax, join classes in folk dancing, singing, languages, or whatever interests them. They form many amateur dance groups, choirs and orchestras. The city is also a great musical centre, with a number of concert halls. The Conservatoire and several music schools produce some of the finest musicians in the world.

Below: The Rossiya Cinema on Pushkin Square.

Left: The Tretyakov Gallery contains a rich collection of Russian art. The pictures range from eleventh-century icons and mosaics, to contemporary paintings. There are also drawings, sculptures and engravings. The building was presented to the city in 1892 by P. Tretyakov, together with his private art collection.
Below: The impressive Ostankino Serf Art Museum.

Left: The Bolshoi Theatre is one of the oldest theatres in Moscow. It was founded in 1776 and can seat over 2,000. It was twice destroyed by fire and was finally restored in 1856. Its columned facade is topped by the famous quadriga of Apollo.

Below left: The auditorium of the Bolshoi Theatre.

Below: The Tchaikovsky Conservatoire, founded in 1866 by the musician Nicolai Rubinstein. Many famous Russian composers and performers were trained here and also taught here themselves. The large hall seats 2,000. A statue of Tchaikovsky stands in front of the building.

A typically colourful performance of opera at the Bolshoi Theatre.

Above left and left: Georgian
national dancers give exciting and
colourful displays.
Above: The Moscow circus is one
of the finest in the world. Its
animals and clowns are highly
trained and perform many feats.
There is also a circus on ice where
bears, as well as humans play
hockey on skates.

Moscow's Open Spaces

Moscow is a very green place, except in winter. This is mainly due to the many parks, gardens and other green spaces all over the city. There are three very large parks and eleven others, most of them accessible by underground or other transport.

Gorky Park is the best known and there are always streams of people entering its gates. Its 300 acres, however, easily absorb large numbers and its amenities appeal to a wide variety of tastes. The park stretches along the bank of the Moskva River for nearly two miles. The further one goes from the entrance, the wilder it grows, with paths winding up the Lenin Hills, among shady trees. These slopes are popular in winter among skiers.

The section nearer the gates is full of flower beds and flowering shrubs. The central path leads to the boating lake, with a cafe on its bank. There is an amusement park with a huge ferris wheel and a parachute jump. There are pavilions for exhibitions and an indoor dance hall. The open-air Green Theatre, with a large stage, can seat 10,000, and there are many other open-air stages for concerts and variety shows. There are dance floors for national and other dancing, cafes and restaurants, all kinds of stalls selling souvenirs, newspapers and ice creams, an outdoor library, chess corners, a rose-garden and seats everywhere.

There are five ponds, including one specially for swans. In winter large areas and paths are flooded to enable skaters to go quite long distances. There are also rinks for children, beginners, and experts.

Sokolniki Park provides many of the same facilities and occupies 1,500 acres. It takes its name from the Russian word for 'falcon' as it was once a hunting forest for the nobility. Large tracts are still wooded and untouched, except for well trodden paths where people come to breathe the fresh untainted air. Beyond the impressive fountain near the entrance is a group of pavilions where international commercial fairs are held.

The third large park is the Ismailova Park, more than 2,000 acres of woodland, streams and meadows. In addition to the usual facilities there is a riding stable and an archery field.

Ismailova was once the Moscow estate of the tsar's family and game was bred in it specially for hunting. Peter the Great spent time here when he was a child and used to sail on the pond.

Another park associated with Peter is Kolomenskoye, once a country residence of the princes and, later, the tsars of Russia. It is on the bank of the Moskva River and is now an open-air museum of Russian architecture. In a grassy meadow is the Church of the Ascension, built by an unknown architect in 1534, and the first Russian church to be put up in the 'tent' style. It is 190 feet high, of red brick and white stone.

A fountain in the attractively laid-out Exhibition Gardens.

Dotted about the park, among the old trees, are various buildings which have been moved from other places, including the 17th century wooden fortress tower from the shores of the White Sea; a tower from the old Bratsk jail in Siberia and a little wooden house from Arkhangelsk in which Peter the Great lived when he was young. At that period he also lived for a time in Kolomenskoye.

The Exhibition of the Economic Achievements of the U.S.S.R. is housed in more than 70 pavilions situated in a vast, well laid-out park. A little rail-less train plies from one end to the other, to save the feet of those who wish to see as many of the pavilions as possible. Throughout the grounds are stalls selling soft drinks, snacks, ice creams and other refreshments; there are also restaurants and cafeterias where full meals are served.

There are other smaller parks in various parts of the city. In addition to these are numerous squares and broad boulevards where seats are always to be found under the trees and by pleasant flower beds.

Below: Sokolniki Park is four times as big as Hyde Park in London. It was formerly a hunting estate for the tsars, who came here with their falcons — sokol means falcon in Russian.

Right: A number of Moscow parks have a special section for children where they can play games, see a puppet show, read or just enjoy the fresh air.

Below right: Playing dominoes in the open air is a popular activity for off-duty Muscovites.

Below and below left: Two of Moscow's beautiful fountains that decorate many of the city's public places.

Above: The Gorky Central Park
rises from the bank of the river up
to the Lenin Hills. One section is
devoted to an amusement park
containing this large ferris wheel.
There is also a parachute jump and
a revolving seat which gives people
brave enough to try the sensation
of going into space.

Left: There are always crowds in Gorky Park, particularly on Sundays, but it is easy to go further into the park and lose sight of them.

Below: Gorky Park has five lakes and there are black swans on one of them. It is also possible to row on the river as there is a large boathouse on the embankment. In winter, vast stretches of the park are turned into skating rinks.

Moscow Excursions

The Arkhangelskoye Estate is a few miles out of Moscow. Here there is a large palace built in the late 18th century; it belonged at one time to Prince Yusupov who was the director of the Hermitage Picture Gallery in St Petersburg. When buying art treasures all over Europe for the imperial collection, he also acquired many for himself. The palace, which is kept as it was when he lived in it, is still full of treasures, pictures by old masters, period furniture and china. The layout of the park was inspired by Versailles. In the park there are other interesting buildings, including a serf theatre, now a museum, and, on a high part of the river bank, a small church which has been beautifully restored. It contains a fine collection of icons.

Zagorsk, a little more than 40 miles from Moscow, is the centre of the Russian Orthodox Church. Priests are trained here and its churches and monastery are among the most famous in the country. The Sergius-Troitsky Monastery was founded in the first half of the 14th century and is an architectural gem. It was also at this time the cultural centre of old Russia. The monastery had an important library, and master icon painters, wood-carvers, silversmiths and other craftsmen had their workshops here. The collection of art treasures accumulated over the centuries can be seen in the museum.

There are numbers of other beautiful churches in Zagorsk, as well as a bell-tower, an old refectory, a hospital, fortress walls and towers, and, a modern touch, a museum of toys with 30,000 exhibits including dolls from many countries and of different periods.

Leninsky Gorky is about 20 miles from Moscow and is the centre of a flourishing collective farm. It is known for the house where Lenin lived at the end of his life and where he died. The house, now a museum, was built in 1830 and stands in extensive grounds. The rooms have been left as they were in Lenin's time. In the garage is the old Rolls-Royce motor car which was given to Lenin by a group of his English friends and admirers.

Although rather far, more than 100 miles, it is possible to visit Vladimir and Suzdal in one day. They are both interesting and beautiful places.

Vladimir was founded in the 12th century and most of it was built by the son of Yuri Longarm. It was enclosed by earthen and wooden fortifications with a Golden and a Silver Gate in them. Many of the cathedrals and churches within this city are standing today and have been fully restored. In the Cathedral of the Assumption there are remains of murals by Rublyov.

Suzdal is preserved as a museum town and contains marvels of old Russian architecture. In the Kremlin, built in the 12th and 13th centuries is the white stone Cathedral of the Nativity. The facade, facing the Kremlin Square, is richly carved and ornamented. Inside, the walls are covered with frescoes from the 13th to the 17th centuries.

The town itself has 36 lovely churches, each one unique in design. There are also many former monasteries and convents. A large tract of land has been turned into an open-air architectural museum. It features old buildings, houses, a well, and a wooden church built without the use of a single nail. They have been brought from many places and reconstructed here.

Two old wooden houses from Moscow have been brought here to form part of the Suzdal out-door architectural museum.

Left: Arkhangelskoye Palace was built in the 18th and 19th centuries and is now a museum that houses a collection of works of art, paintings, furniture and porcelain.
Below: One of the stone lions guarding the palace. These lions have almost human faces.
Bottom: A beautifully restored little church on the Arkhangelskoye estate on the high bank of the Moskva. There is a marvellous collection of old icons on view.

Left: The Pokrovsky Monastery in Suzdal, one of several which are now used as museums.
Below: Snow-covered, wooden houses left from the former village of Pionyskoye. There are still such houses standing in various parts of old Moscow, but they are disappearing fast, giving place to modern buildings.
Right: This old two-storeyed house in the Leningrad district may well be sacrificed to development too.

Below, right and below right: Three
of the many monasteries within
easy travelling distance of the city
of Moscow.

Changing Moscow

Of all the capitals in the world, Moscow has probably gone through the most drastic changes. Since the Revolution of 1917 and especially over the last 15 or 20 years, it has emerged as a modern city with clear outlines for its future development. More than half its population has been rehoused, broad new highways run from the centre, side roads have all been surfaced and one of the best transport systems serves the inhabitants.

Although its vast building projects depend on modern methods and are mainly functional, there have been changes in architectural design. The period when blocks of flats of prefabricated sections looked so monotonously alike, has given way to more variety in size, height, and colour. For example, no longer are all the balconies along a road the same colour. The former dull brown so much used has given way to varied shades. All flats except those on the ground floor have balconies or loggias. At one period in the 1950s five storey blocks, without lifts, were the norm. Now, tower blocks of nine, 12, 20 and more storeys bring variety to the skyline. As practically all the women work and many children are in nurseries and kindergartens until they go to school, the problems of loneliness faced by housewives in tower blocks in other countries rarely arise.

The radial and ring shape of the capital has been extended and developed; the new highways have green boulevards down the middle where people can walk and not suffer from the traffic. Further out they are lined with new modern buildings. The smaller roads off the rings and highways are being brought up to date, and the whole city has been enclosed by a circular bypass, over 67 miles in circumference. Beyond is a green belt, to be used for relaxation.

The first overall plan for the development of Moscow was made in 1935, and all the subsequent plans have been extensions of and improvements to, this plan. As there is no private ownership of land, the City Soviet (City Council) can go ahead without having to buy owners out, or obtain anyone's permission. The next plan was for the years 1951 to 1960, and now the 1971 plan aims to take Moscow into the 21st century, and, as the preamble says, make it a model city. The three zones will remain. The central zone is to continue as the heart of the capital, with many administrative buildings, historic architectural monuments, cultural amenities such as theatres, concert halls, museums and a shopping centre. People will continue to live here so there is no danger of it becoming 'dead'.

The second, middle zone, is still an industrial belt which grew up between the third line of fortifications and the Kamer-Kollezhsky ring during the industrial revolution after the emancipation of the serfs in the 19th century. Railway stations and the river ports are in this area as well as a number of villages and workers' settlements. According to the plan, some industries are to be removed: those which pollute the air or constitute other health or fire hazards. Small factories are to be combined, to leave more space. New shopping centres are being built and green areas planted.

The Panorama Museum contains the vast *Battle of Borodino* canvas — a full 377 feet long and 49 feet high — painted to commemorate the 1812 war. The statue is of the victorious general, Kutusov.

94

The outer zone extends to the peripheral bypass and occupies more than half the area of the city. It includes former small towns and rural settlements. Radial roads are being extended and with them, transport. The underground is being extended further and further out. Here there are many parks and green spaces. Factories, with residential blocks in the vicinity, are being built with the aim of reducing travelling time as much as possible. Many research institutes are going up, as they do not pollute the atmosphere.

It is hoped the plan will ensure that the population of Moscow remains stable by the end of the century at about eight and a half million; that there will be a better balance in the relation between the workplace and home, shopping and recreational facilities. Less industry and more people employed in the public service sector, will make life easier for Muscovites. More schools, hospitals, theatres and cinemas, shops, restaurants and green spaces will be provided. It is possible to believe that this will come to pass, when one sees the pace of development going on now.

Above: Modern apartment blocks now house many of the citizens of Moscow.
Above right: An unusual ring-house block of flats.
Right: One of the new housing estates in Moscow, showing the width of the roads and how the houses are separated from the road by wide verges of grass and trees, as well as by pavement.

Left: The new C.M.E.A. building terminates the reconstructed radial Kalinin Avenue.
Above: A modern Moscow street lined with office blocks. But for the styling of the cars, this street could be in any major city in the world.